The Poems
of
Maria Caridad Lara Sciaky

ೞ ೱ

The Poems
of
Maria Caridad Lara Sciaky

Edited by Albert Sciaky

Photographs by Ramona du Houx

Polar Bear & Company
An imprint of the
Solon Center for Research and Publishing
Solon, Maine

Polar Bear & Company™
Solon Center for Research and Publishing
PO Box 311, Solon, ME 04979, U.S.A.
207.643.2795, polarbearandco.org, soloncenter.org

Copyright © 2016 by Albert Sciaky, Elena Skye, Richard Richter
All rights reserved. No part of this book may be reproduced in any form without permission in writing from the author or publisher, except for brief quotations for critical articles and reviews.

ISBN: 978-1-882190-48-5
Cover design and photographic art by Ramona du Houx.
First print edition, first printing October 2016
Library of Congress Control Number: 2016946724
Manufactured on durable, acid-free paper in more than one country.

Editor's Preface

This is a collection of poems written by my wife, née Maria Caridad Lara, who deceased ten years ago. Maria was a beautiful, bright, creative, and complex woman, but above all she was a poet who loved poetry. Meeting Maria for the first or hundredth time was always notable because she was unique. She had a formidable, almost forbidding presence; her intense attentiveness yet unwillingness to participate in discussions was disarming and to some disturbing; the constant attention she received even from those who didn't know her was puzzling.

The schematic structure of Maria's poetry is very similar and best described by comparing it to a musical configuration called a fugue. A fugue is a polyphonic composition based upon one, two or more themes, which are enunciated by several voices in turn, subjected to contrapuntal treatment, and gradually built up in distinct divisions to a marked climax at the end. Maria's poems enumerate varied themes joined in a contrapuntal format, and like a fugue her poetry is coherent.

As a poet Maria was a classicist, with a flair for mythology, whose research for her poems was exhaustive and encyclopedic. The library in her den included a large assemblage of reference books, which were in constant use. Her poetry collection ranged from Homer, Shakespeare, Chaucer, Milton, Keats to moderns such as Yeats, T. S. Eliot, Emily Dickinson, St. Vincent Millay, Auden, and more. Maria surrounded herself with her literary world.

While reading Maria's poetry, it is important to be informed that she believed she was divulging her personal and private inner self through her poems. That is why she allowed very few, practically no one, to read her poetry. Allowing the reading of her poems was an invitation to intrude into her inner privacy, which privacy she considered sacrosanct. Her daughter and I and an occasional very close friend were the only readers she allowed. Whenever I suggested publishing her poems, she would reply emphatically they were written to document her private thoughts, which thoughts were not intended for public viewing.

Something has to be said about Maria's general attitude towards people to appreciate and to some extent understand her poetry. Maria was tolerant of people she approved and totally intolerant of those she didn't. Her disapproval was exhibited by abrupt dismissals and in lesser matters by ignoring the offending parties. To Maria, disapproval meant exclusion from her presence. Approval meant inclusion in her circle. That was her nature, and she was sufficiently impressive to get away with it. It certainly led to a limited circle of friends and acquaintances. I lived with Maria for fifty years. It made for a challenging and exciting life, not a moment of which I regret.

Something else must said about Maria's inner self to make the depth of her poetry understandable. To those who knew Maria well, it was apparent there were heavy, even dark, concerns on her mind, which she shared with no one, including me, her children, or closest friends. Furthermore, it was apparent that behind Maria's formidable presence there was a fragility. It became very clear to me after she died and I reread her poetry that she had indeed exposed her private inner self and that fragility through her poetry, and for that reason she did not want her poetry shared during her life or after her life.

One of Maria's characteristics I must describe, after the forbidding description of her character above, is her steadfast love and devotion to her children, her grandchildren, and children in general. The love was reciprocal. She encouraged children to read what she called "good stuff." Her selections must have pleased them, as they loved to be with her discussing and reading good stuff. But besides book discussions, Maria would spend long hours with children just chitchatting about the fun things. Children could never get enough of her. When I would ask her why she spent so much more time talking with children than with "grownups," she would respond, because the children are the uncorrupted ones.

Now that it has been ten years since Maria passed away, her immediate family believes the time has come to share her poems. We are not fully comfortable with our decision to publish, but because we consider her poetry uniquely profound and beautiful, we have decided to allow her privacy to be exposed to what Maria would call "public viewing."

Publishing the collected poems of Maria Caridad Lara was made possible by the tireless effort of her daughter, Elena Skye. Elena's husband, David Cogswell, her daughter Rosamund, brother Richard Richter, and myself all contributed a helping hand.

Albert Sciaky

To A.L.S.

When I am in your arms my soul
Lies in a star-encrusted knoll
And all my breath is safely laid
Beside its unfamiliar grade
And my heart in its chamber knows
The scent of the escaping rose
And my eyes in their silk are dressed
When on your loved face they rest

That I might bear your child
I have an Angel's ear beguiled
That I might bear your child
I have grown lilies in the wild

That I might bear your child
On banks of rue and thyme I lie
That I might bear your child
My soul is promised to the sky

Put off your gilded dress and your silk cap
The newly blessed come yourself to wrap in their blithe honor
And their shining halls to show to your bright hair
And worlds so distant that you shall forever wear
A banner of so rare and strange a cloth
That daylight will attract the darkling moth

Maria Caridad Lara Sciaky

Had I a scarlet pin to spend
I would a scarlet flower mend
Had I an emerald to lend
I would a tree in Cyprus tend
Had sapphires fallen in my hand
I would leave heavens in the sand
Had drops of mead rained on my eyes
I would awake in Paradise

One of us with ribbon tape
Take measure of our new life's shape
Let it be you, for you have shown
That awkward contours may dissolve in grace
And one of us must listen for the next note pure
Let it be me, for oh I heard it once
And it was true
And it heralded the brimming sight of you

Love, if you will see me dressed in hyacinth
And with midnight in my hair
Then hurry, the breath of time has chilled my room most perfectly
And every petal lives beyond its bloom
It is unkind that they may not now settle into dust
And that I bear so long the silence of the just

Sweet patriot of the night's sweet gleanings
I hereby disavow my formal leanings
To learn the language of this heavy shore
Oh say no more
Until I can with laughter and with joy
Embrace the flowers you bring
And know their fragrance always wounds this denser air

The air is heavy, thick with love
And does not move, and does not move
A crystal frost is on the ground
It is the crucible of sound

Our breath is measured, cold and rare
And stirs the air, and stirs the air
Now has the golden race begun
Now comes the rising of the sun

There is a just and proper fire
For those who touch the sacred lyre

And she in whom a summer sang
And for whom the steeples rang
Were served an apple laced with rue
But still they raised their voice and do
A sweeter commerce than the blessed
Who lie in Cupid's arms and rest

Dance

For José Carreras

I slept beneath a shower of gold
My soul had shed its gown
And great winds rose and lilies shattered
And lily rain fell on my eyes
And nettles stung my trembling hair
And my breast fell for seven hours
And my hands held it fast again
And in my hands strange flowers bloom
And from my breast new moons are strewn
And in my hair a fulsome night
And in my eyes an agate light

I

I sent another self to you
 Myself to safely keep
 And she came back
 And swept me through
 Then led me to the door

II

Go see how sweetly lies your love
 Amidst the fern and rose
 Amidst the fern and rose he lies
 Though in him pale light flows

III

I ran until I fell amongst
 The frocken where you lay
 I joined by breath with yours again
 And forced another day

Maria Caridad Lara Sciaky

God, thou has let fall an impulse
From thy days of Genesis
And like thee, I love the sturdy light of Sun and Moon
But I love more the voice waiting for happy mischief
Pressing a race beguiled by cyclamen and rose
Into the green declivities of secret snows

Alcestis

I will not lie within the pretty grove
Where the proud king has left his crown
My lips are cold, my skin a winter's down
But oh my eyes, my eyes are bold
And have sent death to linger in the hall
Come husband hold your tranced wife
And see her face make pale a summer's bloom
Come let us lie beneath the Pleiades
Let amorous Orion his great treasure claim

Persephone

Oh whitest silence, greening majesty
If ever any breath escape your lips and on my ear should fall
Tell me how from this vault to discriminate
Rose-golden apples and the glistening bough
And how did you dissemble a fond heart
How can I my misfortune dull some part
Oh sweeter than the violets you let fall
How shall I stand and walk and speak
How my defenses keep

Daughters of Zeus

Resist thy rain and random visits to earth
And pity me
For once, the rapt Mnemosyne distracted by her children
Let fall her footsteps near
And all that had grown soft in me
Hardened into an obsidian stone
Whose fluent crystals I had always known

To Terpsichore

I too am tired of the commonplace
Your face and acquiescent chorus
Has nourished vein and cantilevered leaf
But you shall ever run
Towards the insulting passion of the sun

A king rode by one day
And asked if I would wed
I answered that I would I would though I his purple dread
He bade me drink a glass of mead
And on his soul I fed
Then all my veins were turned to gold
But oh my eyes were lead

Now you must fear the darkness
And I will fear the flame
Together we will answer
The speaking of our name
Who once have periled Hades
The sun can never warm
We seek another country
We are in other form
In this uncharted landscape
We shall need comforting
Then who will bring the mountain
And who the heather bring

I

Angelic beings have painted colors on my brow
That have my voice made soft
As though I speak but in a holy wood
And all my words fly to a greening loft

II

But oh do not put off my tinted cloth
Though sovereign silence lies heavy on my tongue
A sweeter music will repel the moth
Till every note in heaven has been sung

I swear by all the earth's most sweet forbearance
That to preserve your bloom
I would sweep every room in every castle keep
Stir all the waters till they reflect your face
And turn the curse of Venus into grace

There is this about night
Her oblique innocence censors all strategies and mercies
The space you occupy by day is circumscribed and near
But when I sleep
You are abyss, sweet Genesis and Hell

Maria Caridad Lara Sciaky

I have no need of talisman or stone
Your recent alchemy has traced on my breast bone
Inviolate tapestries
No errant stain can mar their sovereign
Nor swell with rain their silver edge
Think that I walk whereon the unicorn has bowed
And know that I am beautiful and proud

Of banners and parapets I know not
  Nor any toilsome thing
But when a wren sings to her love
  She has a purple wing

Maria Caridad Lara Sciaky

The moon when void of course
Is heavy, full
And absently illuminates the night
While Seraphim embrace her in their flight

Maria Caridad Lara Sciaky

Farewell to thy heart's door
To its lintel and its floor
Where nightly my deft footsteps fell
Echoing the shards of Hell
Where etiolated lies
The fond wisdom of my eyes

Heart, by a great wave of love made still, autonomous
Unfit for measured pace
Be now an ornament immersed in ragged streams
For Seraphim to find
Or the exalted blind

Oh twice becalmed Eurydice
Is there a deity
Compassionate and resolute
Can change the chaos of my blood
Into flower, into fruit
Or the dark wine of tap and root
Or drop of mead in silver cup

A pallid substance serves my veins
No golden trace not silver strain
Have I to spend on sun and rain
Cool is the place where I have lain

If rose or crimson had I there
Would dancing be the gown I wear
Would I remove my crown with care
And would my heaven be as fair?

I swear that to this winter's debt
I will add tamarinds that threw their fragrant suns
On sightless ground
And offered like delirious gods
Their acid fruit to the imperial sound

Maria Caridad Lara Sciaky

Not from severe enchantments
Shall Heaven and Hell defend me
But from the gentle scourge of night
Sparrows untended
And from your brief idolatry

The leeward side of August will be mine
Fine and precipitate like wine
Summer will yearn for bright September's leaf
And minarets of snow
The startled rains of April will not know

Sing to me! Oh sing to me
My mouth receive the host
And I shall cap the sweetness in
And you shall have the most

Walk with me! Oh walk with me
Ourselves a mile to gain
Against the pressing mass of green
And the dishonored rain

Lie with me! Oh lie with me
As earth and sky draw near
And make the beating of your heart
The last sound that I will hear

My eyes that have your face made gold
When in your spirit arms you hold
My smaller spirit on your breast
Have seen the last departing guest
Oh singing halls and walls of light
Oh chamber innocent of night
Bring forth your chalice bring it near
I am the only tenant here

Thy holy wound has folded me
Into the fulsome ground
Now be the earth my gallery
And let my grave be sound

So louder than a cymbal crash
So deep in love I lie
That I will keep for leaded sash
The uses of the sky

This strange and fragile little happiness
Has for its breadth an undetermined space
Between a sudden buoyant moment
Irrelevant as waiters at a dance
And a cold wind confirmed to an uncharted land
Futile and spent
That mocks the very name of chance

Maria Caridad Lara Sciaky

I never see the fragile net of spring
Nor toil in any season
Famine and war and every fulsome thing
I think are artless treason
So must you be who tempered my heart's girth
See how we press a hollow in the earth

God-bosomed lovers
Cast a cold eye on me
I am deciduous and keep the seasons close
Never shall any bloom enfold me long
Nor love my winter ever still
Nor still my ravelled fire
Though in him pale light flows

Maria Caridad Lara, by Cecily Diamond

www.ingramcontent.com/pod-product-compliance
Lightning Source LLC
Chambersburg PA
CBHW042007100426
42738CB00038B/121